Where was the Magna Carta signed?

At the bottom

Also by Sylvana Nown

Groans

MORE GROANS

Compiled by
Sylvana Nown

Futura

A Futura Book

First published in Great Britain in 1986 by
Futura Publications
A Division of
Macdonald & Co (publishers) Ltd
London & Sydney

ISBN 0 7088 3150 8

Photoset in North Wales by
Derek Doyle & Associates, Mold, Clwyd
Printed in Great Britain by
William Collins, Glasgow

Futura Publications
A Division of
Macdonald & Co (Publishers) Ltd
Greater London House
Hampstead Road
London NW1 7QX

A BPCC plc Company

Contents

Ouch!

There are good jokes, and there are bad jokes. And there are some jokes that are so terrible you really can't help laughing.

After listening to an avalanche of awful humour – I finally lost count after writhing on the floor pleading for mercy – I have made a selection of the very worst jokes I have ever heard. So bad, in fact, that they sent the needle right off my Groanometer.

The dial on this amazing device begins at belly-laughs and moves through giggles and titters to pained expressions, cries for help, groans and finally hysterical laughter brought on by an overdose of daftness.

If you think you have heard jokes worse than these – and I doubt it – send them to me, and I will award a pair of ear plugs to the winner ... On second thoughts, DON'T send them to me. If I hear any more I'll probably go completely bonkers!

Sylvana Nown

Crazy Customers

Shop assistant: 'Can I help you madam?'
Customer: 'Yes, I'd like a bath for a baby with a galvanised bottom, please.

☆

Customer: 'That horse you sold me last week, fell dead today!'
Dealer: 'Well I told you he had some funny little ways. But I honestly never knew him to do that before!'

☆

Petshop owner: 'Are you looking for anything in particular?'
Old Lady: 'Yes, a fully grown parrot please.'
Petshop owner: 'Well, here's a really good bargain. Only five pounds and it recites poetry, sings *Rule Britannia* and counts to a hundred.'
Old Lady: 'Never mind that, is it tender?'

☆

'Good morning madam. I'm selling vaccum cleaners.'

'Good. Try next door, we use theirs and its terrible.'

☆

'Give me a hat to suit my head.'

'You mean a soft one?'

☆

A man walked up to the bar and asked for a 'Mother in law'.

'That's a new one on me,' said the barman. 'What is it?'

'Stout and Bitter.'

☆

What do you call a Bear that sells insurance?
Winnie the Pru.

☆

The customer in a petshop complained that all the dogs were too expensive.

'In that case,' said the shopkeeper, 'I suggest you go to a Used Cur dealer!'

☆

'Hello, what are you doing at the Chemist's?'

'I want something for my head.'

'Hmmm – how much do you think you'll get?'

☆

The grocer had a box of sweets on the counter and suggested that the little girl take a handful while he was serving her mother. She shyly refused. 'This beats me,' said the grocer, 'I never heard of a little girl who didn't like sweets.'

While he was serving the Mother, he picked up a bag and filled it with a handful of sweets and handed them to the girl. On the way home the mother asked: 'Why didn't you take some sweets in the first place?'

'Because,' answered the girl, 'his hand is bigger than mine.'

☆

A little boy entered a butcher's shop and handed a note over the counter: 'Dear Butcher, please give my Ben a £3 joint of lamb. I cannot come myself as I am in bed with a new born baby and three pork chops.

☆

A butcher was weighing a joint of beef when his customer said indignantly: 'You're giving me an awful lot of bone there, aren't you?'

'Certainly not,' replied the butcher. 'You're paying for it.'

☆

'What kind of meat have you today?'

'We've got mutton and venison.'

'Is the mutton dear?'

'No, the mutton is sheep and the venison is deer.'

☆

'Sorry to keep you waiting, Madam,' said the shopkeeper. 'But my assistant backed into the bacon slicer this morning and I've got a little behind in my orders.'

☆

'How did you manage to get all your Christmas shopping done in one day.'

'I bought the holly first.'

☆

'Do you have a pair of square toed shoes please?'

'No madam, pointed toes are the fashion this season.'

'That may be – but I happen to be wearing last years feet!'

☆

Antique Dealer: 'I have here a very rare revolver. Dates from the time of the Romans.'
Customer: 'But the Romans didn't use revolvers.'
Dealer: 'I know sir. That's what makes it so rare.'

☆

Customer: 'Will the rain spoil this fur coat?'
Assistant: 'Madam, have you ever seen a rabbit with an umbrella?'

☆

Lady: 'A plump young chicken please.'
Butcher: 'Do you want a pullet?'
Lady; 'No thank you, I can carry it in my basket.'

☆

Pretty girl: 'Will this bathing costume shrink?'
Assistant: 'Certainly not, it's very good quality and guaranteed not to shrink.'
Pretty girl: 'Then show me something cheaper.'

☆

Avoiding the toy department of a large store a harrassed mother with a toddler was approached by a determined saleslady. 'Would your little boy like a game of snakes and ladders?' she asked pushing a box towards them.

'Oh, how kind,' said the mother. 'I know he'd love it. I'll just finish my shopping while he plays with you.'

☆

Lady: 'I'd like some crocodile shoes please.'
Assistant: 'Certainly madam. What size does it take?'

☆

Wriggly Giggly

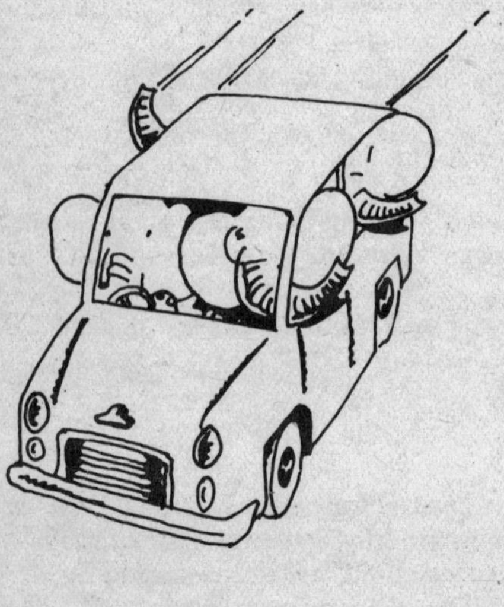

Who held up stages coaches on the sea bed?
Billy the Squid.

☆

Two male centipedes were watching a female go by. Said one male to the other: 'That's a nice pair of legs ... pair of legs ... pair of legs ... '

☆

What did the cod say to the plaice in the fishmongers?
'Hallo there Cyril, long time no sea!'

☆

Two ants were running along at a great rate across a biscuit box. 'Why are we going so fast?' asked one.

'Don't you see?' said the other. 'It says, "Tear along the dotted line".'

☆

Two flies were strolling across a ceiling. 'You know human beings are silly,' remarked the first fly.
'Why do you say that?' asked the second fly.
The first shrugged his wings. 'They spend all that money building ceilings and then walk on the floor.'

☆

Two flies were sunbathing on Robinson Crusoe. As they were about to take off, one said to the other: 'Well, I'll see you on Friday.'

☆

'I say, I say, why haven't you changed the goldfish water?'

' 'Cos they haven't finished last week's yet.'

☆

Which side of a frog is greenest?
The outside.

☆

Why didn't the mother smack the baby moth when he was naughty?
Because she couldn't stand moth bawls.

☆

Ist Golfish: 'I feel terrible this morning.'
2nd Goldfish: 'Then you ought to see a fishician.'

☆

'What did the woodworm say to his friend?'
'Isn't life a bore!'

☆

As a snail climbed up an apple tree, an ant called out: 'Hi, there aren't any apples up that tree.'

'I know,' answered the snail, 'But there will be by the time I get there.'

☆

'Have you fed the goldfish?'

'Yes.'

'Good boy.'
'I fed them to the cat.'

☆

Two snails were making their way across a path when they noticed a slug behind them. 'We're being followed,' said one.
'I know,' replied the other, 'and by a nudist too!'

☆

What's worse than a crocodile with toothache?
A centipede with corns!

☆

Baby snake: 'I'm glad I'm not a poisonous snake.'
Mother snake: 'Why dear?'
Baby snake: ' 'Cos I just bit my tongue.'

☆

What do you call a stupid ant?
An ignorant.

☆

What do you call a bee born in May?
A Maybee.

☆

How do fish learn to count?
On fish fingers.

☆

What do you call a mummy moth?
A mammoth.

☆

A centipede got run over by a lawn mower and lost 98 legs. It struggled to the doctor and asked for a frank opinion. 'Well,' said the doctor. 'I can keep you going for a while yet, but you're definitely on your last legs.'

☆

How does a fish start up in business?
On a small scale.

☆

What is the smallest pole in the world?
A tadpole.

☆

What goes hop hop splash, hop hop splash?
A frog with hiccups.

☆

Why couldn't the butterfly go to the ball?
Because it was a moth ball.

☆

Why did the fly dance in the saucer?
Because it wanted to be presented with the cup.

☆

Why did the mother flea look so sad?
Because all her children went to the dogs.

☆

What do bees do with honey?
They cell it.

☆

Why was the frog banished from the pond?
He kept cracking croaks.

☆

Two mosquitoes were watching blood donors giving their blood. 'Just fancy, they'll lie down and let someone take a pint of their blood, but if we take a nip or two they yell blue murder!'

☆

How do you contact a fish?
Drop it a line.

☆

Comical Crimes

Which criminal is most like a sleeping child?
A kidnapper.

☆

'I can prove my innocence if you'll give me time,' protested the prisoner.

'Right,' said the judge, 'I'll give you five years.'

☆

Warder: 'What do you want to see the governor about?'
Convict: 'Well, I've been here eleven months and I've not heard a word about holidays yet.'

☆

Judge: 'Didn't you think of your poor mother when you stole that suit?'
Defendant: 'Why should I? It's a man's suit.'

☆

Judge: 'Would you prefer to be tried by myself alone or a jury of your peers?'
Prisoner: 'Peers? What's them?'
Judge: 'Peers are your equals. Men of your own kind.'
Prisoner: 'You try this case yourself. I don't want to be tried by a bunch of car thieves!'

☆

What kind of bird can't fly?
A jailbird.

☆

'And what got you into this place?' asked the prison visitor.

'Just plain absentmindedness,' said the prisoner.

'How could that be?'

'I just forgot to change the number plates on the getaway car before I sold it.'

☆

Magistrate: 'You might as well confess to breaking into the fishmonger's. Your suit reeks of fish!'
Accused: But your honour that's not fair! I wasn't wearing this suit when I did it.'

☆

Burglar (caught in the act): 'Just my luck. After spending six months making friends with the dog. I go and tread on the cat's tail!'

☆

What sort of robbery should be without risk?
A safe robbery.

☆

Judge: 'You again! Didn't you promise me last time you were up for stealing chickens that if I let you off you would do better in the future?'
Prisoner: 'That's right sir. This time it's turkeys.'

☆

'Thank you Tommy, I will write and thank your mother for these ten lovely apples.'

'Er ... r r would you mind thanking her for a dozen?'

☆

A bullying barrister was snarling at the witness. 'How far were you from the scene when the accident occurred?'

'Thirteen metres and nine centimetres,' the witness answered.

'How can you say so exactly?' the barrister barked.

'Well I reckoned some fool would ask me that question, so I measured it.'

☆

When the cat burglar reached the sixth floor he stopped and peeped through a window. Inside a toddler was playing with a cuddly toy. The burglar tapped on the window: 'Come and open for your nice uncle,' he said. The toddler stared at him and then said: 'Don't talk like a fool – I can't reach the window yet.'

☆

Magistrate: 'You are a danger to pedestrians. You will not be allowed to drive for two years.'
Defendant: 'But sir, my living depends on it.'
Magistrate: 'So does theirs!'

☆

As the shifty-looking customer prepared to leave the restaurant another diner accosted him. 'Excuse me, but do you happen to be John Smith of Newcastle?'

'No, I'm not,' was the sharp reply.

'Well, I am,' replied the other 'and that's his overcoat your putting on!'

☆

A burglar's son was pestering him for some money for the cinema. 'All right, all right,' grumbled his father. 'I'll get you some as soon as the bank closes.'

☆

A master burglar arranged with a beginner to meet on the job at two a.m. At three a.m. the younger crook slipped through a window in Riverside Drive and whispered: 'Harry? Are you there, Harry?'

'Yes you fool,' Harry whispered back. 'I said two not three a.m.'

'I know Harry,' said the youngster, 'But you didn't say which number. I've been breaking into them all to find you.'

☆

Judge: 'Have you ever been up before me?'
Accused: 'I don't know your honour, my usual time is 7.30 a.m. for breakfast at 8.00 a.m. What's yours?'

☆

Magistrate: 'You are charged with stealing a tortoise.'
Prisoner: 'I didn't steal it, honest guv. It followed me home.'

☆

'What is your occupation?' asked the magistrate.

'I'm a locksmith, sir,' replied the prisoner.

'Then what were you doing in that bank when the police were called?'

'I was making a bolt for the door.'

☆

'The judge had to let that deaf man off.'

'Why?'

'Because the law says you can't convict a man without a hearing.'

☆

Judge: 'Gentlemen of the jury, have you come to a decision?'

Foreman: 'We have, your honour. The jury are all of the same mind – temporarily insane.'

☆

What type of thief steals meat?
A beefburgler.

☆

What happened when a film was shown in the prison?
It was a cell-out.

☆

Why aren't prisoners allowed to swim?
In case they produce a crime wave.

☆

Judge: 'Order, Order in court!'
Prisoner: 'Fish and chips please.'

☆

Exexutioner: 'Any last request?'
Condemned man: 'A bottle of wine please.'
Executioner: 'Very well – any special kind?'
Condemned man: 'Er yes, a 1999 vintage please.'

☆

'Were you relieved when the burglar left?'

'Very, I was relieved of a watch, a ring, a necklace … '

☆

A man charged with stealing appeared in court with no legal advisor. 'How does it happen that you have no representative?' asked the judge.

'Well I did engage a solicitor,' explained the suspect, 'but as soon as he found out that I had not stolen the £20,000, he dropped my case.'

☆

A little old lady was held up on the street by a burly thug armed with a revolver. 'You ought to be ashamed of yourself, holding up a poor little old lady like me,' she said. 'A man your size ought to be robbing banks!'

☆

Judge: 'You plead guilty to stealing this man's coat and now you want your fine reduced?
Accused: 'Yes, I had to have the sleeves shortened.'

☆

What did the policeman say to the clothes shop burglar?
'You're under a-vest.'

☆

What do you call a judge with no thumbs?
Justice fingers.

☆

Did you hear about the lorry load of wigs stolen on the M1?
Police are combing the area.

☆

Who sat in a bubble bath solving crimes?
Sherlock Foams.

☆

Belly Laughs

What kind of pie do cannibals like best?
Snake and Pigmy.

☆

The mother tiger came down the jungle path and saw her fierce half-grown cubs chasing a disarmed hunter around a bush. 'Children,' she scolded, 'How many times do I have to tell you it is bad manners to play with your food?'

☆

Colonel to new cook: 'What did you do in the War, my man?'
Cook: 'Officers' cook sir, Wounded twice.'
Colonel, sampling soup: 'You were lucky, I wonder they didn't kill you.'

☆

Which kind of fruit was most plentiful on Noah's Ark?
Pears.

☆

'What's that?' asked the young son of a cannibal as an aeroplane passed overhead.

Unperturbed, his father replied: 'It's something like a lobster – you only eat what is inside.'

☆

What do you get with instant food?
Instant indigestion.

☆

Hear about the trouble in the biscuit factory last night? A Bandit punched a Penguin and was chased by a Trio in a Taxi. United, they caught him and were awarded Blue Ribands by a Viscount at his Club.

☆

'Do eat up, I've taken great pains over this cucumber salad.'

'I know, I've caught 'em!'

☆

How do you get electric eggs?
Buy a battery hen.

☆

What kinds of food do geese eat?
Gooseberries.

☆

What do channel swimmers train on?
Currants.

☆

What's the main cause of being overweight?
Living hand-to-mouth, hand-to-mouth, hand-to-mouth …

☆

What's the origin of ice cream?
Frozen cows.

☆

The cannibal chief had been in bed for several days and even the witch doctors couldn't find what the trouble was. 'He doesn't seem to get any better,' sighed his wife, 'I just don't know what to make of him.'

'Don't worry,' said her neighbour. 'I'll lend you my new recipe book.'

☆

'Mum, mum, can I have a drink of orange juice?'

'No – we've none left. Have a drink of water, it's good for your blood.'

'But mum, I'm not blood thirsty.'

☆

Mother: 'You didn't ask for a second piece of cake did you?'
Child: 'No, that's bad manners, mother. I just took two pieces the first time.'

☆

Boy: 'What did you do in the war, Grandad?'
Grandad: 'I saved the lives of 5000 of my comrades.'
Boy: 'Gosh – how?'
Grandad: 'I shot the cook.'

☆

First cannibal: 'Am I late for dinner?'
Second cannibal: 'Yes, everybody's eaten.'

☆

Is it better to swim on a full stomach – or an empty one?
Neither – it's better to swim on water.

☆

Which is the best way of storing fresh milk?
In a cow.

☆

How do you start a rice-pudding race?
Sa-go!

☆

What would you do if you swallowed your knife and fork?
Eat with your spoon, of course!

☆

What do you call a monk who cooks fish?
A frier.

☆

What do you call a monk who serves in a chip shop?
A chip monk.

☆

Neighbour: 'Here is a piece of cake for you, Michael.'
Michael: 'Thankyou.'
Neighbour: 'I do like to hear children say, Thankyou!'
Michael: 'Give me a couple of more pieces and you can have a grand time!'

☆

First Chief: 'What did you make of the white missionary?
Second Chief: 'Hot at the week-end and cold on Monday.'

☆

What did the baby say to the lollipop?
'I can lick you anyday!'

☆

'Well, so long,' said the mouse, waving goodbye to the hunk of cheese, 'Nice to have gnawn you.'

☆

How do you make a hot-dog?
Sit it in the sun.

☆

Which table can't you eat off?
The multiplication table.

☆

What did the oven say to the casserole?
I can make things hot for you.

☆

How do you make gold stew?
With 18 carrots.

☆

What keeps hot in the fridge?
Pepper.

☆

'Have you ever had an apple turnover?'
'No, but I've had one roll away.'

☆

Why did the tomato cry?
It couldn't ketchup with the rest.

☆

1st man: 'My wife treats me like an idol.'
2nd man: 'How's that?'
1st man: 'She gives me burnt offerings every night.'

☆

Why do children like watching T.V. in the morning?
Because breakfast cereals are a good way to start the day .

☆

Why were the little biscuits so sad?
Because their father had been a wafer so long.

☆

Comical Couples

Marry in haste and repeat at leisure.

☆

What did the boy-owl say to the girl-owl on a rainy night?
'Too-wet-to-woo.'

☆

How does a conjuror propose marriage?
'Will you be my wife, to halve and to hold?'

☆

'My Uncle's got a wooden leg, and it hurts him like anything?'
'How could a wooden leg hurt?'
'My Auntie hits him over the head with it.'

☆

Husband: 'This ointment makes my back smart.'
Wife: 'Would you like me to rub some on your head?'

☆

Prison Officer: 'Come on Jake. Your wife's bailed you out.'
Convict: 'That's just like her. She never lets me finish a sentence!'

☆

She: Would you put yourself out for me?'
He: 'Of course.'
She: 'Then shut the door as you go.'

☆

'There must be visitors downstairs.'

'Why?'

'Because I've just heard Mummy laugh at one of Daddy's jokes!'

☆

He: 'You know, there are just two things that stand in the way of my becoming the best male dancer in this club.'

She: 'I know, your feet!'

☆

'The Sultan's son is inclined to be a bit naughty at times.'

'Harum scarem?'

'Oh no, he's used to them.'

☆

Did you hear about the manicurist who married a dentist?

They fought tooth and nail.

☆

'When I get married I'm going to have six children.'

'When *I* get married I'm going to have dozens of children.'

'Aw, that's an awful lot of kidding.'

☆

Roses are red,
Violets are blue,
Orchids are expensive,
Will dandelions do?

☆

When is a room full of people empty?
When they're all married because there's not a single person there.

☆

Boyfriend: 'Is your father rich?'
Girlfriend: 'He's got so many gold teeth he has to sleep with his head in a safe.'

☆

'Couldn't you care for a chap like me?'

'Yes, if he wasn't too much like you.'

☆

A well-to-do vicar advertised for a butler and next morning a well-dressed young man rang the bell. 'Can you run the bath and get breakfast ready for seven o'clock?'

'I expect so,' said the young man.

'Can you polish the silver, wash the dishes and keep the house tidy?'

'Say vicar, hold on,' said the young man. 'I came here to see about getting married, but if it's going to be as much work as all that, you can count me out now!'

☆

'Simon, why have you bitten Polly?'

''Cos she said she was made of sugar and spice and everything nice – but she tasted horrible to me.'

☆

Husband: 'Unfortunately, I ran over Tompkin's dog, but I've promised to replace him.'
Wife: 'Don't be silly – you can't bark!'

☆

She: 'I've heard an awful lot about you.'
He: 'Perhaps – but you can't prove it.'

☆

Husband getting out of bed after a thunderstorm the previous night. 'Did you hear the storm last night, Mary? Thunder and lightning and all.'

'Well, why didn't you wake me up? You know I can't sleep when it thunders.'

☆

What is a bachelor?
A man who never Mrs a woman.

☆

He: 'Here is your engagement ring.'
She: 'But this diamond has a flaw in it.'
He: 'You shouldn't notice that – we're in love and love is blind.'
She: 'Not stone blind!'

☆

When does Cleopatra flirt?
When Julius Caesar.

☆

Wife: 'Why don't you bring me chocolates now that we're married?'
Husband: 'Did you ever see someone keep feeding worms to a fish after it's caught?'

☆

Husband looking around at a party: 'It's odd, but the biggest idiots always seem to marry the prettiest women.'
Wife: 'Oh, now you're trying to flatter me.'

☆

Boy: 'I'm a very enthusiastic person, I can't help throwing myself into everything I do.'
Girl: 'Good. So go and dig a deep hole.'

☆

Besotted daughter to her Dad: 'Harry is awfully clever, he's got brains enough for two.'
Dad: 'Good. You'd better marry him then.'

☆

Which piece of furniture suits a tall girl?
A tallboy.

☆

Girl: 'I found a pound on the way to school today.'
Boy: 'Oh, I think it's mine. I dropped a pound and couldn't find it.'
Girl: 'But I found two fifty-pence pieces.'
Boy: 'Then it's definitely mine. I thought I heard it break when it hit the pavement.'

☆

Which girls should boys avoid?
Miss Chance, Miss Chief, Miss Take, Miss Hap, and Miss Fortune.

☆

Young man: 'Sir, I want to marry your daughter.'
Film Star's Father: 'Can you divorce her in the manner to which she has been accustomed?'

☆

'What would you do with a thousand pounds, if I gave it to you?'

'Count it.'

☆

'I like her taste in perfume.'

'I see – you're led by the nose.'

☆

Early one morning, a milkman on his round was startled to see a spaceship swoop down and land in the middle of the road. A hatch opened and several little green men climbed out. They began to scan the area with field glasses. Leaving his float, the milkman cautiously approached the little green men. 'Excuse me,' he said. 'But what are you fellows looking for?'

Without lowering his field glasses, one of the little green men replied: 'Little green women, stupid.'

☆

Young medical student: 'It would be wonderful to be ill and to be nursed by you.'
Nurse: 'It would be a miracle actually, I'm on the maternity ward.'

☆

Loony Lessons

Who was Joan of Ark?
Was she a relative of Noah's?

☆

What does a sculptor do?
Makes faces and busts.

☆

What is the future of 'he drinks'?
'He will be drunk'.

☆

Where was the Magna Carta signed?
At the bottom?

☆

What do you think e.g. is short for?
Egg sample?

☆

What is M.D. short for?
Mad dog?

☆

Where are Kings and Queens of England crowned?
On their heads.

☆

How can you tell the difference between the male and the female skeleton?
The female's is the one with the open jaw.

☆

Who invented fractions?
Richard the Third.

☆

Why did the flea fail his exams?
He just wasn't up to scratch.

☆

Hear about the mathematician with a glue problem?
He got stuck on a sum.

☆

Maths teacher: 'In the Smith family there are Mother, Daddy, and the baby. How many does that make?
Pupil: Two and one to carry.'

☆

Teacher: 'Your son spells atrociously.'
Parent: 'Very good, I can't even spell that myself.'

☆

Teacher: 'Why did you leave your last school?'
Pupil: 'Illness, miss. The teacher got sick of me.'

☆

Teacher: 'Now I hope you understand the importance of punctuation.'
New Pupil: 'Oh yes, sir, I always come to school on time.'

☆

Teacher: 'William, pay attention at once. Now what happened when King John came to the throne?
William: 'Please sir, he sat down.'

☆

'I don't want to scare you,' little Joey said to his teacher, 'but my Dad says that if I don't get a better school report, someone is going to get a good spanking!'

☆

Name six Arctic animals.
Three polar bears, two seals and one reindeer.

☆

What did the Israelites do when they came out of the Dead Sea?
They dried themselves off.

☆

'Give me one sentence making use of the word nitrates.'

'Night rates are cheaper than day rates.'

☆

What is man's chief end?
The one with the head on.

☆

What is the opposite of evergreen?
Never green.

☆

What other minerals exist in England besides coal and iron?
Lemonade and ginger beer.

☆

'Who came first out of the Ark?'

'I don't know sir, but I do know that Noah came forth.'

☆

Which famous breed of cattle comes from the Channel Islands?
The cow.

☆

What do you know about Queen Victoria's subjects?
That they're all dead.

☆

Which kind of insects are most likely to attend school?
Spelling bees.

☆

What is the capital of the Isle of Man?
The money they get from tourism.

☆

Why was the maths book so upset?
He was full of problems.

☆

Give the definition of:
Nudism ... A lot of fuss about nothing.
Art ... Just a pose.
Adam ... A man you don't know other people from.
Home ... A place where you moan most and get treated best.
Dignity ... Something you stand on when you take things lying down.

☆

When was the Iron Age?
Before drip-dry.

☆

What is the most important thing to remember in chemistry?
Don't lick the spoon!

☆

What do kids want most out of school?
Themselves.

☆

A student at college was taking a course in birdwatching. On the fifth day they had a test on 50 different species of birds. When the student received the test paper showing only the birds legs and feet, he exclaimed: 'I don't remember studying this!'

The professor replied: 'I'm sorry, but you have automatically failed this course, please leave immediately.'

As the student was walking out, the professor asked him: 'By the way, what is your name?'

The student stopped at the door and slowly pulled up his trouser legs and then shrewdly remarked: 'You tell me!'

☆

What is the definition of Summer Holidays?
The teacher's no bell peace prize.

☆

Alphabet Noodles

Why is the letter E so sad?
Because it isn't in good spirits.

☆

What is in December but not in any other month?
The letter D.

☆

What is a niche?
Something you scratch.

☆

Two cockney soldiers were writing home, and one asked the other: 'How do you spell "fought", Bill?'

'Which "fought" do you mean?' asked Bill. 'The fight you fought, or the fort you fight in?'

'I don't mean either, you idjit,' was the reply. 'I mean the fought you fink!'

☆

What appears once in every minute, twice in a moment, yet not once in a year?
The letter M.

☆

Which word is always pronounced wrong?
Wrong, of course!

☆

Where does Monday come before Sunday?
In the dictionary.

☆

What is the longest word in the dictionary?
Smiles – because there is a mile between the first and last letter.

☆

Which letter of the alphabet is most like an island?
The letter T – because it is in the middle of water.

☆

Which letter is a vegetable?
P.

☆

How do you make an witch scratch?
By taking away her W.

☆

If your luck isn't what is was, write a P in front of it and try again.

☆

What is the centre of gravity?
The letter V.

☆

Primitive Weapons	by A.P. Shooter
Tea and Sympathy	by Mona Lotte
Prehistoric Animals	by Terry Dactile
How To Make Money Quickly	by May B. Owinn

How To Keep Appointments	by Cal Endar
Sewing for Beginners	by N.E. Stitch
Training Racehorses	by Ivor Looser
How To Deal With Garden Pests	by D.D.T. Spraye
Lessons in Horseriding	by M.T. Saddles
Games and Competitions	by U.R. Owte
How To Improve Your Hearing	by Isabel Ringinn
Making Friends	by C.U. Later
What To Do In Your Spare Time	by T.D. Umm
Monkey Tricks	by B.A. Babboon
Practical Jokes	by M.A. Peste
Desert Trail	by Rhoda Cammel
Famous Counterfeiters	by Dud Money
Early Training	by A. Potte
Racing Cars	by Rory Ferrari
Great Hoaxes and Frauds	by A. Fiddler
Stamp Collecting	by Penny Black
Lamps and Lampshades	by Shanda Lear
The Law And Your Rights	by S. Windle
D-I-Y Tips	by Andy Mann
You And Your Diet	by Henrietta Lotte
Trying To Be Good	by Ernest Lee
Surprise Tricks	by Major Jumpp

Whistle While You Work ...

Boss: 'Can you write shorthand?'
Secretary: 'Yessir, but it takes me longer.'

☆

'Look at this letter,' snarled the boss. 'Why can't you type things as I say them?'

'Because my typewriter hasn't got a cold.'

☆

'Are you one of those workers who watch the clock?'

'No sir, I have a watch with a built in alarm, set for hometime.'

☆

Actress: 'Tell me, does my new part do me justice?'
Playwright: 'Yes, I should think so, you die in the first act.'

☆

A bricklayer at the top of a partly built house shouted to the foreman that he could not find his way down. 'Come down the way you went up,' shouted the foreman.

'Not on your life,' he yelled back. 'I came up head first!'

☆

1st Farmer: 'What did you give that horse of yours when she was ill?'
2nd Farmer: 'Turpentine.'
(One week later)

1st Farmer: 'What did you say you gave your horse when she was ill?'
2nd Farmer: 'Turpentine – I told you last week.'
1st Farmer: 'But my horse died!'
2nd Farmer: 'What! Well now, so did mine!'

☆

Cub Reporter: 'How shall I write this story about the doggy hero?'
Editor: 'Oh, make it snappy.'

☆

Why is hanging wallpaper an absorbing occupation?
Because you can get really wrapped up in it.

☆

Why was the bow-legged cowboy sacked?
Because he couldn't get his calves together.

☆

In a hotel kitchen which cook wears the largest hat?
The one with the biggest head, of course!

☆

What kind of man has to shave at least twenty times a day?
A barber.

☆

A reporter opened his notebook and waved his pencil at a man just leaving the lion's cage. 'Are you the famous liontamer the whole town is talking about?'

'Not likely. I'm only the chap who cleans their teeth and brushes their manes!'

☆

There were a group of men talking at a party and one asked: 'How's business?'
Author: 'Mine is all write.'
Tailor: 'Sew sew.'
Butcher: 'Pretty lean.'
Coalman: 'Not so hot.'
Optician: 'Looking brighter.'

☆

Matron: 'When I was young I loved dancing, but I took up nursing and spent all my spare time studying. And that's how I became what I am today.'
Student: 'One of the world's finest nurses.'
Matron: 'No. One of the world's worst dancers.'

☆

He was an excellent chauffeur, and kept the car absolutely spotless, but he was rather careless about his own appearance. Mrs Rich decided she would have to speak to him about it. As she settled into the seat beside him she spoke: 'Robert,' she said, 'how often do you think it necessary to shave?'

Robert looked at her: 'With a weak growth like

yours, madam,' he said politely, 'I should think about once every three days would be sufficient.'

☆

Employee: 'I've come to complain sir, someone's started a silly rumour that I'll be leaving the firm.'
Boss: 'Yes, well it was me, actually.'

☆

Which type of men shave most carefully?
Policemen – they don't want to nick themselves.

☆

Why did the cowboy take his saddle to bed with him?
In case he had a nightmare.

☆

Which is the most violent profession to follow?
Cooking – because you beat eggs, whip cream, chop vegetables and crush herbs.

☆

Why couldn't the sailors play cards?
Because the Captain was standing on the deck.

☆

'Is he a steady worker?'

'Well if he was much steadier, he'd be motionless!'

☆

'I can't allow these long telephone calls,' said the manager.

'Er, this was business,' replied the secretary.

'Oh, and which of our clients were you addressing as "sweetie"?'

☆

Which kind of job drives customers away?
Taxi driving.

☆

1st Man: 'I'm a great comedian.'
2nd Man: 'How do you know that?'
1st Man: 'I put some of my jokes in the fire, and it just roared!'

☆

1st Butcher: 'The Queen buys her meat from me!'
2nd Butcher: 'God Save the Queen!'

☆

What do you call a crocodile hunter?
A snap-shot.

☆

What can a clumsy cook make best?
Drop scones.

☆

Why did the liontamer stick his left arm down the lion's throat?
He'd already lost his right one.

☆

Which kind of suit would a banker choose?
One with checks.

☆

What did the executioner's wife say when he changed his coat?
'Oh, you're forever chopping and changing!'

☆

Nervous employee to boss: 'Your son has made a dreadful mistake, sir.'
Boss: 'My son wouldn't make a stupid mistake like that. It must have been some other fathead.'

☆

Customer: 'Two pounds for two simple questions. Expensive isn't it?'
Fortune Teller: 'Yes dearie. Now what's your second question?'

☆

'I haven't much time for meals,' said the bus driver, 'so I generally have a bite at the wheel.'

'That must be rather tough,' said his listener.

☆

A job was vacant at the circus. 'Our monkey has died,' said the manager to Jones. 'Will you put on a monkey skin and impersonate him for the Christmas season?'

While Jones was capering about as a monkey a performing lion growled viciously at him and Jones yelled for help. 'Shut up!' growled the lion, 'Or you'll get us all the sack!'

☆

A shop assistant became tired of his job and joined the Police Force. Meeting a friend one day he was asked if he liked his new job. 'The hours are satisfactory, the pay is good, but best of all, the customer is always wrong.'

☆

Sergeant-Major: 'When did you blow in?'
New Recruit: 'I came in with the last draft, sir.'

☆

Clumsey obtained a job as a packer in a china wholesalers. On the third day, he smashed a big and valuable vase. On pay day he was summoned to the manager's office and was told that half his wages would be deducted each week until the vase was paid for.

'How much was the vase worth?' he asked anxiously.

'About five hundred pounds,' replied the manager.

'Hurrah!' shouted Clumsy.

The manager asked him why he was so happy.

'Well,' said Clumsey, 'it looks as if I've got a steady job at last.'

☆

What did the midwife say to the postman?
'I'm in the delivery business myself.'

☆

Two missionaries were standing together in a cannibal's cooking pot. One turned to the other and said: 'Never mind. At least this will be their first taste of religion.'

☆

Fortune teller: 'I can see a dreadful disappointment for someone very near to you.'
Client: 'That's right! I've come out without my purse, and can't pay you.'

☆

Manager: 'I'm sorry, I can't have your act on here. I never allow boisterous language in my theatre.'
Comedian: 'But I don't use boisterous language!'
Manager: 'No – but the audience will if I put you in the show!'

☆

A farmer had a son who left the country for the city, where he took a job as a french polisher.
Now the farmer makes hay while the son shines.

☆

Foreman: 'What are you limping for?'
Workman: 'I've got a nail in me boot.'
Foreman: 'Why didn't you take it out?'
Workman: 'What – in me dinner hour?'

☆

What did the actor say when he got a plateful of sponge and custard in his face?

'That was a trifle unexpected.'

☆

An explorer back from Darkest Africa was showered with questions about his adventures. 'Is it true,' someone asked, 'that if you carry a torch the wild animals will not harm you?'

'That depends,' smiled the explorer, 'on how fast you carry it!'

☆

Artist: 'Shall I paint you in evening dress?'
Lady: 'Oh no, my dear chap, don't make any fuss at all – just wear your overalls.'

☆

What did the astronomer say when he discovered a new star?

'Business is looking up.'

☆

Cannibal chief: 'What did you do for a living?'
Victim: 'I was an assitant editor.'

Cannibal chief: 'Cheer up, after tonight, you'll be editor-in-chief.'

☆

Some soldiers were having their first lesson in parachute jumping. 'What if the 'chute doesn't open?' asked one.

'That,' said the instructor, 'is jumping to a conclusion.'

☆

Boss: 'We're looking for a responsible man.'
Applicant for job: 'That's me all right! Everywhere I've worked, if anything went wrong, they said I was responsible.'

☆

The stage manager was trying frantically to prevent the stubborn unfunny comedian from going in front of the curtains to take his bow. 'Listen to them booing,' said the manager.

'But there is some clapping among the booing,' retorted the unperturbed comedian.

'Yes,' snapped the exasperated manager, 'but that's for the booing!'

☆

Frantic Postman: 'Call your dog off!'
Houseowner: 'That's no use, he'll only answer to Rover.'

☆

Why did the tightrope walker always carry his bank book?
To check on his balance.

☆

If a sword swallower went on a diet, what would he eat?
Pins and needles.

☆

What makes a professional chess player happy?
Taking a knight off.

☆

What kind of clothes do solicitors wear?
Law suits.

☆

Why was the farmer hopping mad?
Somebody trod on his corn.

☆

Mr Butcher is six foot tall, he wears size ten shoes and exercises every day. What does he weigh?
Meat.

☆

Why was the carpenter so annoyed when he hit the nail?
'Cos it was his thumbnail.

☆

Why did the bank manager become bored?
Because he lost interest in everything.

☆

What is an astronomer?
A night watchman with a degree.

☆

Taffy was working on a turning lathe in the village factory, when he was caught in the main belt of the machine which took him round and round. After he had gone round three times he was thrown to the ground. His mate dashed up to him and cried: 'Are you all right, Taff?'

'Why are you so interested?' asked Taffy in a huff. 'I just passed you three times and you hid your face in your hands.'

☆

It was one of those days when there was nothing doing in the bank in a small Irish town. The staff had got through the day somehow with tea and talk, until it was time to close. 'Three o'clock!' said the manager at last. 'Run and close the front door Binns.'

The junior returned in a few moments and said: 'Excuse me, sir, it is closed. We forgot to open it this morning.'

☆

Boss to retiring employee: 'Well Davidson, what have you got to say after thirty years with the Post Office?
Davidson: 'Don't mail my pension.'

☆

Officer: 'Are you happy now that you're in the army?'
Soldier: 'Yes sir.'
Officer: 'And what were you before you joined up?'
Soldier: 'Much happier, sir.'

☆

Police sergeant to young cadet: 'Suppose someone approached you with a sharp knife, what steps would you take to protect yourself?'
Cadet: 'Long fast ones, sir.'

☆

A dog walked into a pub and asked the bartender for a drink. 'I'll have the usual, Joe,' he said.

'The usual? I serve six hundred drinks a day and you expect me to remember "the usual"?'

☆

How do you spot a hairdresser at a football match?
He's the one waving his hair.

☆

What happens when a hairdresser gets the 'flu?
He just wants to curl up and dye.

What's Up Doc?

Patient: 'Doctor, Doctor I need help. I keep thinking I'm a dog, and I've got into the habit of barking at visitors.'
Doctor: 'How long have you been thinking like this?'
Patient: 'Since I was a puppy.'

☆

Glassworker: 'Quickly doctor, I need your advice. I was blowing glass and I breathed in. What do you think will happen to me?'
Doctor: 'Oh I expect you'll get panes in the stomach.'

☆

A woman and her husband rushed into a dentist's surgery. 'I want a tooth pulled,' the wife said. 'Don't bother with the gas, we're in a hurry.'

'You are brave,' said the dentist. 'Which tooth is it?'

'Jack,' the woman said, turning to her husband, 'Show him your tooth!'

☆

Joe told the doctor, 'I have terrible dreams in which I turn into a fish.'

'Nothing to worry about,' said the doctor. 'Many people have that kind of dream.'

'But doctor,' cried Joe. 'I can't swim.'

☆

'Rheumatism,' said the doctor, 'causes a man to imagine that his joints are very much larger than they actually are.'

'I know,' exclaimed Mrs Smith, 'our butcher has it!'

☆

The nervous patient sat in the dentist's chair twisting her handkerchief in anxiety. 'I understand,' she murmured, 'that you extract teeth painlessly.'

'Most of the time it doesn't hurt a bit,' said the dentist, 'but the other day I sprained my wrist.'

☆

Two regular women patients were chatting in the doctor's waiting room. 'I didn't see you here last week, Annie.' remarked one of them. 'I do hope you weren't ill!'

☆

A doctor had a call from a father whose son had swallowed his fountain pen. 'Be right along,' said the doctor. 'What are you doing in the meantime?'

'Using a felt-tip.' said the father.

☆

'Doctor, a terrible thing has happened to me. I think I've lost my memory.'

'How long has this been going on?'

'How long has what been going on?'

☆

'Doctor – I think I'm shrinking again.'

'Well, you'll just have to be a little patient once again.;

☆

Dentist: 'Now Billy what would you say to a small filling?'
Billy: 'Can't I have a large one – I'm starving.'

☆

Two psychiatrists were discussing their cases. 'One of my most unusual cases is a patient with a split personality,' said one.

'That's not very unusual,' replied the other.

'This one is,' said the first. 'They both pay!'

☆

A patient with a split personality visited a psychiatrist. 'Doctor,' he said, 'you'll have to help me get some sleep. I go to bed quietly at ten and sleep for a couple of hours. Then, just after midnight, my noisy rowdy self starts shouting and swearing and my meek side wakes up. I can't get a wink of sleep and I go to work exhausted.'

'Hmmm,' said the psychiatrist after deliberating. 'Tonight, try a little experiment. Sleep in separate rooms.'

☆

Doctor (replacing the telephone): 'I must go and see Mr Ramsbottom.'
Wife: 'Will you be coming straight home when you've seen it?'

☆

'Hello, Doctor, I'm Milligan.'

'Oh, well where exactly does it hurt?'

☆

Patient: 'Am I crazy if I talk to myself?'
Doctor: 'No, but you are if you listen.'

☆

Doctor: 'Mrs Smith we have discovered that your bad temper is caused by an ugly little microbe.'
Mrs Smith: 'Hush, not so loud doctor, he's next door in the waiting room.'

☆

Mother's little boy refused to eat. In desperation, she took him to a doctor, who tried to tempt the lad with talk of good food. Unsuccessful, the doctor threw up his hands and said: 'All right, what would you like to eat?'

'Worms,' replied the boy.

Not to be outsmarted, the doctor sent his nurse out for a plate of them. 'Here,' he shouted at the boy.

'I want them fried,' he wailed. Again the nurse went out and returned with a big plate of fried worms.

'I only want one,' yelled the boy. The doctor got rid of all but one. 'Now,' he bellowed, 'Eat.'

'You eat half,' insisted the boy. The doctor forced down half the fried worm, then dangled the remaining portion in the boy's face. The boy started crying again.

'Now what's the matter?' growled the doctor.

'You ate my half!'

☆

Doctor: 'Have your eyes ever been checked?'
Patient: 'No, I don't think so. They've always been plain brown.'

☆

'Doctor, doctor, there's a terrible pain in my shoulder.'

'Right, take off your coat and I'll have a look at it.'

'Tell me the worst, doctor – is it rheumatism?'

'No – your braces are twisted.'

☆

Doctor: 'Have you been taking those pills I prescribed?'
Patient: 'No doctor, the box said take one on retiring and I'm not sixty for another six months.'

☆

The doctor made a house call to look in on Grandma who was getting over a chest cough. After a minute or two he ran downstairs and popped his head round the door and asked for a screwdriver which the astonished family gave to him. He emerged again and asked them for a hacksaw. When on the third occasion he wanted a hammer the amazed daughter cried: 'Is everything all right doctor?'

'Not yet,' he growled. 'But it will be when I get this counfounded bag of mine open.'

☆

Dentist: 'Has this tooth ever been filled before?'
Victim: 'Nnnnooo.'

Dentist: 'Well its very queer, because I find small bits of gold on my drill.'
Victim: 'Very likely, I think you've struck my earing!'

☆

'I've just been having an argument with the dentist.'

'Who won?'

'It ended in a draw.'

☆

Patient: 'Doctor, I'm afraid I'm losing my hair, every time I comb it it comes out by the handful. What can I do to keep it?'
Doctor: 'Take this paper bag and fill it three times a day.'

☆

When do you need toothpaste?
When your teeth are loose.

☆

What's the similarity between a garage and a dentist's?
They are both filling stations.

☆

Who don't mind when you pull tongues at them?
Doctors.

☆

'Doctor, doctor I think I'm a window!'
'Just tell me where your pane is.'

☆

'Doctor, doctor I think I can fly.'
'Oh, come down to earth!'

☆

'Doctor, doctor I feel like a dustbin.'
'Don't talk rubbish.'

☆

'Doctor, doctor I feel like a pair of curtains.'
'Then pull yourself together.'

☆

'Doctor, doctor I think I'm a duvet.'
'You need a good shake.'

☆

'Doctor, doctor, I feel like a letter.'
'Well pop through, and I'll open you up.'

☆

'Doctor, doctor, I think I'm a tea-towel.'
'Oh, dry up!'

☆

Doctor: 'And how do you feel today?'
Patient: 'With my hands, as usual.'

☆

What's funny about being in hospital?
An operation – it leaves you in stitches.

☆

My sister thinks she's a chicken. We would take her to the doctor, but we need the eggs.

☆

Wife: 'What are you doing tearing those pages out of your book?'
Doctor: 'Sorry dear. They're labelled "Appendix" and I took them out without thinking.'

☆

'Doctor, do you think vegetables are healthy?'
'Well, I've never heard one complain.'

☆

Fortune Teller: 'There is money coming to you, and I can see no sickness whatever.'
Client: 'That's strange, I'm the new doctor.'

☆

Party Hostess: 'Won't you do something to amuse the guests doctor? Everyone else has performed.'

Doctor: 'Certainly. I'll order that last singer to bed for a month.'

☆

Doctor: 'What are you so wound up about?'
Patient: 'I've swallowed my watch.'
Doctor: 'Then, it's time to go, old man.'

☆

Dentist (off for a game of golf): 'If anyone asks for me this afternoon, Miss Smith, tell them I'm busy filling eighteen holes.'

☆

'You know,' said the doctor, 'the source of your trouble is this ear.'

'This 'ere what?'

☆

Dentist: 'Have you seen any small boys ring my bell and run away?'
Passerby: 'They weren't small boys – they were adults.'

☆

'After my operation the surgeon discovered he'd left a sponge in me.'

'Do you get any pain?'

'No, but I get terribly thirsty.'

☆

A patient consulting a psychiatrist paid in advance and signed his cheque 'Napoleon'. Asked by the psychiatrist why he did this, he replied: 'If I signed my real name, would I need you?'

☆

A young man went to his doctor complaining of insomnia. The doctor finding nothing wrong with him advised him to start counting when he went to bed and to go on until he fell asleep. The following day he was back in the surgery. 'Well,' said the doctor, 'Did you follow my advice?'

'I did,' replied the patient. 'I actually got up to 453, 975.'

'And then you fell asleep?'

'Oh, no, doctor! Then it was time to get up.'

☆

The patient was a judge, and he was very nervous. Just as the dentist had finished the injection to freeze his gum, the judge stopped him. 'Before you go any further,' he said shakily, 'I want you to raise your right hand and solemnly swear to pull the tooth, the whole tooth, and nothing but the tooth!'

☆

Doctor: 'And how do you feel today?'
Patient: 'A little better, but my breathing is bad.'
Doctor: 'We'll soon put a stop to that.'

☆

Doctor: 'You're coughing a lot better this morning, young man.'
Billy: 'I ought to be, I've been practising all night.'

☆

After giving the patient a full medical examination the doctor explained his prescription as he wrote it out. 'Take the green pill with a full glass of water after getting up. Take the red pill with a full glass of water after lunch and the blue pill with a full glass of water after dinner.'

'What exactly is my problem, doctor?' asked the patient.

'You're not drinking enough water.'

☆

Psychiatrist: 'Now we've completed all the tests, I actually think you are a bit crazy.'
Patient: 'I demand a second opinion!'
Psychiatrist: 'Okay, I think you're ugly too!'

☆

Psychiatrist: 'Why are you so annoyed? You're now completely cured.'
Patient: 'Annoyed? Of course I'm annoyed, when I came in here I was Louis IV of France, and now I'm just a nobody!'

☆

Holy Smoke

Why was the vicar walking on his hands?
Because it was Palm Sunday.

☆

What did the vicar say when the church caught fire?
Holy smoke!

☆

Vicar: 'After the blessing the Bishop will leave, and we will all sing 'Now Thank We all Our God.'

☆

Doctor to Vicar: 'Do you talk in your sleep?'
Vicar replies: 'No, Doctor. I talk in other peoples'.'

☆

A vicar's sermon was being interrupted by the snores of a man in the front pew. Wishing to embarrass him he whispered: 'All those who plan on going to Heaven, will please rise!' After they had sat down again, he shouted: 'Now all those who deserve to go to Hell will rise!'

Startled into wakefulness the sleeping man jumped to his feet. His glanced at the seated congregation and looked at the standing vicar and said: 'Well, Reverend, it looks like it's just you and me!'

☆

Where can a small boy hold up a train without getting into trouble for it?
At a wedding.

☆

Sunday School teacher: 'Now children, you must never do anything in private that you wouldn't do in public.'
Small boy: 'Hurrah! No more baths.'

☆

'I understand,' said the vicar's wife, 'that the new building opposite the Mission Hall is to be a public house.'

'A public house?' said the vicar. 'My dear, we *must* go into that!'

☆

Two little children were talking outside their Sunday School. 1st child: 'We're up to original sin.'
2nd child: 'That's nothing, we're past redemption!'

☆

How long did Cain hate his brother?
As long as he was Abel.

☆

'Now,' said the vicar to his Sunday School class, 'Can any of you tell me the name of an immense place where huge pillars rise high above you; where there is soft music and delight and where we all go to if we are good?'

'The cinema!' chorused the class.

☆

A dam burst and mountains of water cascaded into the valley. A minister preoccupied with writing his sermon, didn't become aware of the danger until water swirled into his church study. He fled upstairs and looked out of the balcony window. A group of people in a boat called out: 'Reverend! Reverend! Come with us!'

But he shook his head and said: 'The Lord will save me.'

As the rising water forced him onto the roof, another boat passed by and again the occupants called for him to get in. And again he replied, 'No, thank you. The Lord will save me.'

As he was driven to the top of the bell tower, a third boat passed and offered assistance. 'No, go on,' he said. 'The Lord will save me.'

The water engulfed the church and the next thing the minister knew, he was standing before St. Peter at the Pearly Gates. 'Why Reverend Davis,' St. Peter said surprised. 'What are you doing here?'

'Well I'm not really sure,' replied the minister. 'I trusted in the Lord and I thought He would save me from the flood.' St. Peter looked exasperated. 'Well,' he snapped. 'We did send three boats!'

☆

Vicar to the Sunday school class: 'If I gave one of you two apples and told you to give one to your brother, which would you give him, the big one or the little one?'
Jones: 'That would depend on whether you meant my big brother, or my little one.'

☆

Criss Cross Quiz

What do you get if you cross a hedgehog with an octopus?
A brush with eight handles.

☆

... if you cross an electric blanket with a toaster?
People who pop out of bed.

☆

... when you cross a pig with a pair of spiked running shoes?
A porcupine.

☆

... when you cross a parrot with a cracker?
Awful jokes!

☆

... when you cross a rabbit and a spider?
A hare-net.

☆

... if you cross an orange with a comedian?
Peels of laughter.

☆

... if you cross an owl with an oyster?
Pearls of wisdom.

☆

... if you crossed an elephant with a mouse?
You'd get big holes in your floorboards.

☆

... when you cross a ghost with a cow?
Vanishing cream.

☆

What do you get when you cross an elephant with a kangaroo?
Pot holes all over Australia.

☆

... when you cross the Atlantic with the Titanic?
Halfway.

☆

... when you cross a tree with a genius?
Albert Pinestein.

☆

... when you cross a Japanese car with the morse code?
Datsun dashes!

☆

... when you cross a rose with a camel?
Hard to say, but I wouldn't try smelling it!

☆

… if you cross a bean with a rifle?
Beanshoots.

☆

… if you cross a lawn with a helicopter?
Lots of little greenflies.

☆

… if you cross a dog with a chicken?
Pooched eggs.

☆

… if you cross a shark with a parrot?
An animal that can talk your leg off.

☆

Tee-hee Riddle-me-ree!

What has two hands but cannot feed itself?
A clock.

☆

How many sides has a windmill got?
Two – inside and outside.

☆

What runs but cannot walk?
Water.

☆

What has a head but no face?
A nail.

☆

Why are bricks like eggs?
Because they have to be laid.

☆

What have a millionaire and a baker got in common?
Loads of dough.

☆

What can you keep when you give it away?
A cold.

☆

When is a man like a snake?
When he's rattled.

☆

What is placed on a table and cut but never eaten?
A deck of cards.

☆

Which is heaviest, a full moon or a half moon?
A half moon 'cos a full moon is lighter.

☆

Which kind of dog feeds the hand that bites it?
A hot-dog.

☆

Where is the best place to find a helping hand?
At the end of your arm.

☆

Lots of stools have four legs, so why does a milking-stool have only three?
We can only suppose it's because the cow has the udder!

☆

When is a square a ring?
When it's a boxing ring.

☆

When is a mouse like a pony?
When it is in a trap.

☆

Why are days like suitcases?
Some people seem to pack more into them than others.

☆

What has four legs but only one foot, and one head but no neck?
A bed.

☆

When is a dress like a chair?
When it is satin.

☆

Which part of a clock is never brand new?
The second hand.

☆

What has ears but cannot hear?
A field of corn.

☆

What goes round a garden without walking?
A fence.

☆

If March winds bring April showers, and April showers bring May flowers, what do May flowers bring?
Hay fever.

☆

What is the opposite of cock-a-doodle-do?
Cock-a-doodle-don't.

☆

Wally Mixtures

Pat and Jack were standing beside a river one night, trying to think of a way to cross it. Mack came along with a flashlight and said: 'I'll shine a beam of light across the river and you two can walk across on it.'

Pat turned to Jack and said: 'Does he think we're stupid or something? We'll get halfway across, and he'll turn off the light!'

☆

Wise men say 'Since the right side of the brain controls the left side of the body, left handed people are the only ones in their right mind.'

☆

How does a farmer stop a cockrel from crowing early on Sunday morning?
Eat it on Saturday night.

☆

There was a blind man who went into a department store with his guide dog. He picked up the dog and started swinging it around by the tail. The dog was barking and carrying on. So finally the manager approached him and asked if he wanted any help. He said: 'No thanks, I'm just looking around.'

☆

Do you know what a thief is?'
A person who finds something before it gets lost.

☆

'His mind is wandering but he doesn't care – it's too small to go far.'

☆

Business man: 'When I started in life I'd hardly a shirt on my back, and now by sheer hard work, I've made over a million.'
Bored Listener: 'But surely you can't wear them all.'

☆

A good curse to put on somebody: 'I hope in your next life you're a centipede with ingrowing toenails and corns!'

☆

A scientist had perfected a space camera which could photograph the entire earth. It was sent into orbit and returned to earth.

'How was the picture?' reporters asked.

'No good,' was the reply. 'Someone moved.'

☆

'I can't sleep at nights.'

'I can give you a cure. Imagine you're on a tightrope a thousand feet above ground. You go along it, step by step ...

'Yes?'

'Then you'll drop off.'

☆

What did the nurse say to the patient she was wheeling to the operating theatre?
'Now aren't you lucky – you're going to the theatre to attend an opening.'

☆

Lady: 'Excuse me, but can you direct me to the Moneymost Bank?'
Tramp: 'Lady, do I look like a bank director?'

☆

Chairman of the Old Boys' Association: 'Good evening, professor. I didn't expect to see you here. I thought you weren't coming to our dinner.'
Professor: 'As a matter of fact, my boy, I had decided not to come, but I forgot.'

☆

A cinema has been converted into a skating rink. It still seats just as many people.

☆

Why is the cemetery the most popular place in town?
Because everyone is dying to go there.

☆

Two duellists agreed to fight it out at dawn.
One said: 'If I'm a little late don't wait for me g-g-go ahead and shoot.'

☆

Why are some people like wheelbarrows?
No use unless pushed.
Why are some people like canoes?
They drift around unless paddled.
Why are some people like kites?

They fly away if you don't keep them on a string.
Why are some people like balloons?
They're full of wind.
Why are some people like wristwatches?
They're always at hand.

☆

An old blind man had been selling laces at the same spot for years. Every day a well-dressed man passed, put ten pence into the box, but never took a pair of laces. One day, the blind man stopped the businessman. 'Are you the kind gentleman who puts ten pence in the box every day,' he asked, 'and never takes any laces?'

'Yes, I am,' said the businessman.

'Well,' said the blind man, 'They're up to twelve pence now.'

☆

'You gave that cloakroom attendant a pretty good tip.'

'Well, he gave me a pretty good coat.'

☆

'Good heavens! Cannibals!'

'Now, now don't go getting in a stew.'

☆

'Why have you let Ginger join your gang? He's such a dreadful bore.'

'I know – we wanted someone to grumble about.'

☆

'How do you like your new digs?'

'The food is so-so, but the gossip is great.'

☆

An angry old gentleman watched the naughty boy from next door throwing stones at his cat.

'Hey you!' he called, 'I'll teach you to throw stones at my cat!'

'Thank you sir,' was the grateful reply. 'I've been trying for half an hour and I haven't hit him yet.'

☆

Simple Simon was greatly worried about where the sun went when it went down. He used to stay awake at night pondering on this.

Then it finally dawned on him.

☆

A veteran aircraft carrier was in port on exhibition to the public. On its flight deck was an inscribed bronze plague. 'And here,' said the guide solemnly, 'is where our gallant admiral fell.'

An elderly woman piped up: 'And no wonder! I nearly tripped on the silly thing myself!'

☆

A little boy went into the bookshop and asked for a volume in the window entitled *Advice to Young Mothers.* With raised eyebrows, the assistant asked why he wanted such a book.

He replied, 'I'm collecting moths.'

☆

Alfred: 'That's a terrible scar you've got on your forehead.'

Algie: 'Oh, next to nothing, dear boy, next to nothing.'
Alfred: 'Yes, I know, but it's still an awful scar.'

☆

'What was Lord Nelson famous for?'

'His memory.'

'What makes you think that?'

'Well, they erected a monument to it didn't they?'

☆

'Be careful not to fall here – it's very dangerous,' cautioned the mountain guide. 'But remember,' he added, 'If you do fall, look to your right – there's a wonderful view.'

☆

'When were you born?' asked the sergeant.

'December 1962, sir.' answered the recruit.

'Ah,' mused the sergeant, 'It was a bitterly cold winter that year.'

'I'll say,' echoed the recruit. 'Why, I was brought by a penguin – the stork couldn't make it.'

☆

Outside a cinema in wartime ...
'I'm sorry madam, you can't be admitted without your gas mask.'

'Don't worry about me, I have no sense of smell.'

☆

'You must think I'm a perfect idiot.'

'Well, perhaps not perfect, but you're doing quite well.'

☆

Cannibal cook: 'Am I to boil the missionary, chief?'
Cannibal chief: 'Don't be silly, that's a friar!'

☆

For some time the two women sitting in front of him at the cinema had annoyed him with their constant chatter. Unable to stand it any longer he leaned forward and said, 'Excuse me, but I can't hear.'

'I should hope you can't,' replied one woman coldly. 'This conversation is strictly private.'

☆

'Well,' said the egg in the monastery, 'out of the frying pan and into the friar.'

☆

When a naval ship called at a port in India, the captain allowed some of the crew ashore, but warned them they must be back on board by nine p.m.

Nine o'clock came but no member of the crew had returned. Hours later they started drifting back. Each gave the same excuse that he had left town in time, but being unable to get a taxi, had hired a horse-drawn native vehicle. On the way back, the horse in each case had dropped dead. The captain listened patiently as each of the crew told his story, until the last one was brought before him. Then he exploded: 'Don't tell me – you caught a horse-drawn carriage and the horse fell dead.'

'Oh no,' the last seaman replied. 'I caught a taxi

all right, but I couldn't get here for dead horses.'

☆

'Mum, what's a tongue twister?'
'That's when your tang gets all tungled up.'

☆

When some people promise to be on time, it carries a lot of wait.

☆

What did the big firecracker say to the little one?
'My pop is bigger than yours.'

☆

A bird in the hand is ... ?'
Bad table manners.

☆

Newspaper Reporter: 'Good morning, Madam. You have won five thousand pounds cash, ten pounds a week for life, a world cruise and a pet dog!'
Winner: 'What breed?'

☆

'Hey boy, what are you doing up my pear-tree?'
'Well sir, there's a notice below which says, 'Keep off the grass!'

☆

'The tailor said my suit is a perfect fit.'
'It looks like a convulsion to me.'

☆

" 'Scuse me lady, could you give a poor fellow a bite?'

'Sorry, I don't bite myself – try next door, they've got a dog.'

☆

What does it mean if the barometer suddenly falls?
It wasn't nailed up properly.

☆

'Jim failed his parachute test today.'

'Oh, he fell short, eh?'

'No. He went the full 15,000 feet.'

☆

Sherlock Holmes: 'Ah my dear Watson. I see you have on your summer underwear.'
Watson: 'Marvellous, Holmes, marvellous! How ever did you deduce that?'
Holmes: 'You've forgotten to put on your trousers.'

☆

What has no feet but wears out many pairs of shoes?
The pavement.

☆

'It says the enemy are using seasoned troops. What does that mean?'

'They're mustered by their officers and peppered by us.'

☆

An old lady and her husband fell down a well. Why was the old lady first to get out?
'Cos she had a ladder in her tights.

☆

What do you get if you swallow a teacup?
A bad case of hic-cups!

☆

What kind of ship never gets wrecked?
Friendship.

☆

A professor and a farmer were travelling together, and the professor suggested asking riddles to pass the time. 'Everytime you fail, you give me a pound,' he said, 'and everytime I fail, I'll give you one.'

'You're better educated than I am,' replied the farmer. 'I'll give you 50p.'

The professor agreed, and the farmer asked: 'What has three legs walking and two legs flying?'

The professor gave up and handed over a pound. The farmer said that he didn't know either and gave him 50p.

☆

What is a twip?
A twip is what a wabbit takes when he wides a twain.

☆

Caller: 'Come quickly – there's a fire in my house!'
Fireman: 'How do we get to your house?'

Caller: 'Don't you still have that big red truck?'

☆

'Mummy, Mummy, the puppies are here!'

''Have you seen them?'

'No.'

'Then how do you know?'

'The dog is empty.'

☆

A visitor to a nudist camp noted one nudist with a beard that reached to his knees.

'What's with the beard?' asked the visitor.

'Well,' came the answer, 'someone has to go out for coffee.'

☆

A lady complained to the telephone operator that she had been cut off while talking to her son.

'Did he call you, madam?' the operator asked.

'Oh no,' the lady replied. 'He always calls me, "mother"!'

☆

Dad bought his son a new boomerang for Christmas – and the kid went crazy trying to throw the old one away.

☆

Little Herbert groaned aloud when the lions rushed into the arena and attacked the slaves during a film about Ancient Rome,. He began to get really agitated when the lions started to eat the slaves.

'Don't be scared son, – it's only a movie,' said his Dad soothingly.

'But it's not fair!' Herbert cried.

'I know,' Dad said, 'but don't get upset, it's only a film.'

'Yeah, – but look at the poor lion in the centre – he hasn't even had a bite yet!'

☆

A king wanted to send a message to another kingdom. So he sent a page out on horseback to deliver the message. But before the page got to the other kingdom a gigantic hand with yellow fingers came down and captured him.

Finding this out the King sent another page on foot, telling him to walk as silently as he could. The page tiptoed to the other kingdom and the hand didn't hear him.

The moral is: Let your pages do the walking through the yellow fingers.

☆

Masseurs – People who knead people.

☆

Weight Watcher's Award: Nobelly prize.

☆

Two leather-clad bikers brought their motorcycles to a halt at the zebra crossing. A nun with her arm in a sling, crossed in front of them. 'Hey, what happened to you?' asked one of the bikers.

The nun explained she had slipped in the bathtub and broken her arm.

As they rode on, one biker asked the other, 'What the heck's a bathtub?'

'How should I know,' said the second. 'I'm not a catholic!'

☆

Mum: 'What did you do at the party dear?'
Lisa: 'We sang the refrigerator song.'
Mum: 'How does that go?'
Lisa: 'Freeze a jolly good fellow ... '

☆

Newsboy: 'Extra! Extra! Read all about it – two men swindled.'
Man: 'Give me a paper, boy. Hey, there isn't anything here about men being swindled!'
Newsboy: 'Extra! Extra. Three men swindled!'

☆

A visitor to a factory that manufactures computers asked what went on behind a door marked 'Superstars.'

'Oh,' said the guide, 'that's a special department where they are working on very advanced models. We have one that is almost human.'

'You mean,' asked the visitor, 'that it can correct its own mistakes?'

'Well not quite,' replied the guide, 'but it will blame its mistakes on other computers.'

☆

Mother: 'Why are you making faces at that bulldog?'
Small boy: 'Well, he started it!'

☆

'Don't act like a baby!'

'I can't help it – I was born like that.'

☆

'No two people on earth think alike.'

'You'll change your mind when you see your Christmas gifts.'

☆

Jones: 'I dreamed last night that I was being kicked by a horse.'
Brown: 'It must have been a nightmare!'

☆

'Did you ever have an accident!'

'No, but last year a bull tossed me over a fence.'

'But, don't you call that an accident?'

'No. The horrid beast did it on purpose!'

☆

'Can you lend me a fiver for a week, old man?'

'Who's the weak old man?'

☆

'This match won't light.'

'What's the matter with it?'

'I dunno – it lit all right a minute ago.'

☆

'This dog is worth £500!'

'Coo! But how could a little dog like that save so much money?'

☆

Bald Man: 'You should charge less for cutting my hair.'
Barber: 'We don't charge for cutting it – we charge for the time spent looking for it!'

☆

Book-keeping is the art of not returning borrowed books.

☆

'This party's really boring I think I'll clear off – are you coming?'
'I'd love to, but I can't.'
'Why not?'
'It's my party.'

☆

Transparent means something you can see through – a key hole for instance.

☆

'Name the four seasons.'
'Salt, pepper, mustard and vinegar.'

☆

What is a civil war?
When each side gives way a little.

☆

Farmer: 'Have you any seats left?'
Theatre box office: 'Only stalls and boxes, sir.'

Farmer: 'What do you take me for – a cart horse?'

☆

At the pantomine a lady and a party of children were returning to their seats after the interval. 'Did the children trample on your toes as they went out?' she asked a man at the end of a row.

'Yes they did,' he replied expecting an apology.

The lady turned to the children: 'Come on kids, this is our row.'

☆

How do you know a sound sleeper?
By their snores.

☆

What do you call a person whose hobby is watching the stars?
A movie fan.

☆

Customer: 'I wonder can you help me out?'
Bank Manager: 'Certainly sir, the door's on your left.'

☆

What would you do if you were in my shoes?
Polish 'em.

☆

1st Boy: 'Hear the one about the worm in the cornfield?'
2nd Boy: 'No.'

1st Boy: 'I'm not surprised, it goes in one ear and out of the other.'

☆

Which is friendlier, the sea or the land?
The sea, it waves.

☆

Two buckets met in the street:
1st bucket: 'You're a little pail.'
2nd bucket: 'Yes, I'm not a well bucket.'

☆

Why is a calendar useful when crossing the desert?
You can eat the dates and get water from the spring.

☆

Hear about the two big holes in the ground?
Well, well!

☆

'You've got three holes in your pants!'
'Where?'
'Where you get into them.'

☆

Where do aristocrats go for a night out?
To a knight club of course!

☆

Two eggs were in the 'fridge. One egg said to the other: 'It's cold in here.'

The other said: 'Wait 'till you get outside. First they'll crack your head open, then they'll scramble your brains.'

☆

Why is a clock on the stairs dangerous?
It might run down and strike one.

☆

Why did the tramp keep his eye on the sky?
To see if there was any change in the weather.

☆

Which poets are buried at Poet's Corner in Westminster Abbey?
Dead ones.

☆

Which bad habit can you continue after death?
You can lie still.

☆

Did you hear about the Irish Banana Factory that went bust?
They threw away all the bent ones!

☆

Head Bangers

How long is the average shoe?
One foot.

☆

If a pointed nose indicates curiosity what does a flattened one indicate?
Too much curiosity.

☆

Her teeth were like pearls ... scarce.

☆

'You can try to get up today Jason.'
'But my leg still hurts.'
'That's a rather lame excuse.'

☆

'Mrs Brown, Mrs Brown, I've cured Tommy's lisp!'
'Oh, good boy! How did you do it?'
'I knocked his front teeth out.'

☆

When is a long face like a biting wind?
When people turn their backs on it.

☆

'How did George break his leg?'
'Well, you see those steps over there?'
'Yes.'
'Well, George didn't!'

☆

It has been reported that a million people are overweight.

Of course, that's just a lump sum.

☆

Bather, bather, burning bright,
Seeking for new sides to fry on,
How you're going to wish tonight,
You had saved a side to lie on.

☆

What did the right eye say to the left eye?
'Just between us, something smells.'

☆

'My Gran's got teeth like stars.'
'How's that?'
'They come out at night!'

☆

What can be knitted without knitting needles?
Your brows.

☆

Why do people laugh up their sleeves.
Because that's where their funny bones are.

☆

Fat man to thin man: 'You look as though there's been a famine!'
Thin man to fat man: 'Well, it's obvious you caused it.'

☆

How do you get rid of water on the knee?
By wearing pumps.

☆

Why does a hole in the tooth feel so big on your tongue?
It's just the natural tendency of the tongue to exaggerate!

☆

'Toes reveal a person's nature.'

'How did you find that out?'

'By treading on a few!'

☆

'A fellow just told me I looked like you.'

'Oh did he? Where is he? I'd like to knock his head off.'

'You're too late. I've just killed him.'

☆

Barber: 'You're hair is thinning. Have you ever tried any of our special hair treatments sir?'
Customer: No, I can't blame it on them.'

☆

How does a hairdresser say goodbye.
She gives you a wave.

☆

1st Soldier: 'I told my mum that since I joined the Army I'd grown another foot – so she sent me an extra sock!'
2nd Soldier: 'That's nothing, I told mine that my voice had dropped – so she sent me a chin-strap!'

☆

What did the sock say to the foot?
'You're putting me on.'

☆

What is not human but has four fingers and a thumb?
A glove.

☆

What could you do to try to grow a beard?
Buy a tin of 'Whiskas'.

☆

Why were the tonsils excited?
Because the doctor was taking them out that night.

☆

How did you get that black eye?
I got hit by a guided muscle.

☆

What has a tongue but cannot speak?
A shoe.

☆

What's the cure for water on the knee?
Drainpipe trousers.

☆

What is a wig?
Ear-to-ear carpeting.

☆

Punk: 'Why are you massaging my scalp?
Hairdresser: 'I'm not. I've lost my scissors in there.'

☆

What is a quick cold?
It's when you have a racing pulse and a running nose.

☆

Where do you go to get your ears pierced?
A disco.

☆

What did the tie say to the hat?
'You go on ahead, I'll hang around here.'

☆

Why are your nose and your chin never friends?
Because words pass between them.

☆

'Mummy Mummy, my new shoes hurt.'

'That's because you've got them on the wrong feet.'

'But Mummy, I haven't got any others!'

☆